"Do you remember"

By Mary Carolan

Contents

*Sincere thanks to my family and friends,
who were so helpful & supportive.
Also Lee & Elizabeth, BDA*

Do You Remember
Memories of bygone days

The title of this was inspired by school friends when ever we meet. Every sentence starts, "Do you remember"

For instance;
Do you remember when we played "Baby House" in the shed with broken cups, plates and pretend food, inviting our friends in for a tea party. They had to bring sweets to pay for the privilege.
Going to school and calling for all our friends on the way, sometimes having to wait while they got up and had their breakfast.
Sitting down on the roadside in order to copy homework, sometimes getting caught by the teacher who drove that road to school.
If we arrived without some friends who stayed in bed, the teacher would send one of us to fetch them before roll call.
How important we felt when the teacher left us in charge of the class.
Our school was a semi-detached building, consisting of two rooms each, one half for Boys and the other half for the Girls.
Junior Infants, Senior Infants, 1st and 2nd classes in one room with 3rd, 4th, 5th and 6th classes in the other. Just two teachers for each room boys and girls.
Overcrowding was never mentioned. The teacher we had in junior classes was pretty easy going but the lady for senior classes liked to use the cane a lot on her bad days , which she seemed to have a lot of. We had ways of repaying her for this, one was to have a boy from the

other end come and tell her that the master would like to see her. We sat quietly while she did her hair and makeup before going next door. Only to find out it was a hoax. We felt justified when she came back looking like a beetroot and embarrassed.

She really liked to impress the inspectors when they called. For weeks before his visit she tried to have us word perfect in every subject and anyone unlucky enough to fail the test had sore hands for weeks afterwards.

Sharing the occasional cigarette. The first person took it out to the toilets (outdoor shed) and lit up, when they finished it was left in a hole in the wall for the next person. Sometimes we passed it over the wall for the boys to have a smoke.

Considering the conditions we had, we came away from school with a pretty good education which prepared us for the big world because most of us had to go straight into employment at fourteen years of age, as soon as it was legal to leave school.

Secondary education was only for people who could afford the fees either as a day pupil or a boarder. We are now told that our school days were the best days of our lives: we didn't think so at the time.

The Hill

I was born and raised in a very caring neighbourhood on a little road called "The Hill" at the bottom end of a small market town in County Cavan.

There were approximately thirty four houses in total on the hill and at the time it seemed very normal but looking back it was the best place a child could learn about life.

A breakdown of the occupants of these houses were: two postmen, five factory workers, three farmers, four guards, one bread delivery man, two carpenters, one blacksmith, two fowl dealers, two farm labourers, two dressmakers, one greyhound breeder, one shop owner, three teachers, one bicycle repairer, one harness repairer, one watch repairer, one solicitor, one horse dealer, one butcher, one midwife and "The Pump".

So, as you can see, it was a very self sufficient area and a wonderful place to live. There were approximately sixty four children in the community. Boredom was unheard off as was class discrimination. The road was always full of kids out playing games every day, with no door closed to us. This rule was respected and obeyed, if you called for your friends and homework was being done or it was dinner time, you were just asked to come back later. We were always allowed into the forge and the carpenters work shop to watch them at work.

When the hens and turkeys were been got ready for sale, the children were welcome to pick up the feathers and place them in bags. The feathers were later used to fill mattresses and pillows. The same applied to the farmers, especially at harvest time when we could help with the hay and the potato picking.

Everyone who lived on the hill deserves the story of

their lives to be told, but unfortunately I am not the one to do it. But a few examples that have stayed in my mind are the following.

The bread delivery man who travelled to nearby towns bringing fresh "Spicers" bread to all. He started with a pony and trap for transport and eventually was promoted to a van. As well as supplying all the shops he stopped at all houses in between the towns. He brought tea, sugar, bacon, sausages and the weekly "Celt" which contained all the local news.

One of the Guards was the "school guard", part of his duty was to visit all schools in the area at least once a month to check the roll books. If he found that any child was missing from school often he then visited the parents and issued a warning. If it continued they could be summons before the court and fined.

At least one of the factory workers had his horse and cart employed by the same factory where he worked. This was a factory that made building bricks. The horse and cart was used for the transport of the bricks from one yard to another.

The midwife was a lovely lady and everyone's friend, as well as delivering all the babies she often provided food and clothes for them, she knew all the children by name. When a death occurred on the hill, she was usually the one who would help with the "laying out" and the funeral arrangements.

One house where everybody was welcome day or night was the one with 10 children.

Bridget was a mother in a million, not only to her own but to children from all over the town. Her son caught rabbits by setting traps at night around the farm and went out early in the morning to collect them. Some were sold to provide extra income, but she also cooked some and when they were pot roasted they tasted unique. I don't know how she did it but there was always plenty for anyone who called in. You didn't have too book in advance. As I said before they were wonderful people willing to share whatever they had with each other.

Transport for the postmen were bicycles, how they got all the letters delivered everyday is hard to imagine as they would stop and "story tell" in every house. They always had sweets for the children as well as the post he brought the latest news from town to country.

One famous item that stood halfway up the hill was "the pump". This was situated off the road with a wall built around it and was the only source of fresh water for the residents of the town.

The water came from a well through the pump and was very important. We as children loved to walk the wall around the pump, but were sure to get punished if we were caught messing with the water.

The water wasn't plumbed into houses but had to be carried by can and bucket every day. It was one way for children to earn pocket money by fetching it for the elderly people.

Houses on the Hill
(Do you remember?)

As you entered the top of the town and looked down the hill it would be obvious that an architect hadn't designed the houses. Buildings of all sizes and shapes were there. Most homes were built on one side of the road. Starting with the pub on the corner, which had a dwelling house attached and a two storey house in the same unit. These each had small gardens behind them and a footpath in front. Next came a terrace of five houses, one large and four smaller ones. They also had back yards where pigs and hens were kept and a footpath separated the front gardens from the houses. Some gardens provided potatoes and vegetables, others flowers. Two fields separated these houses from the next block. This consisted of three two story houses that had high walls around them. After that there stood a cottage type house with a thatched roof, an open street, a few fields and sheds, then a large house enclosed with hedges and trees growing in the front garden. A bungalow separated this from the following two houses which had garages attached. These were built beneath road level. A wall surrounded them and they had steps from the road down to them.

More fields followed which were used for growing hay. Then there was a block of four houses. One was the shop, it had a large window and a flat roof, which made it look smaller that the others. Three sets of semi-detached houses ended that side.

On the opposite side of the road, starting at the town's end, stood a lovely bungalow with out houses and large gardens front and back, it always had beautiful flowers around it. More fields after that and then four cottages.

Just one more house that the local butcher lived in which had a abattoir at the back. Then a large farm and "The Pump" with a wall all the way down to the farm house. This was a very big house with out houses, a wide open street and fields with an orchard all round it. Next came a single house enclosed by trees and hedges.

The last house on that side was built high up from the road, with ten steps leading up to it. It was a beautiful house with an arch over the door and small windows. There were lots of large trees around it and gardens to the side and back. A row of cherry trees grew over looking the road and that was the end of the Hill.

As they were all built at different times people just built the size of house they wanted and as some had more land than others, the houses were different shapes also.

These houses lasted for hundreds of years. Most are still there, with others having been added over the years. None of them had water on tap, but that didn't stop them being clean. Cleanliness was very important to everyone. People had ways of collecting rain water in tanks and barrels placed beside the houses with drain pipes bringing the water from the roof into them. Water for use indoors was carried from the pump.

When children arrived from school or play, hands and faces had to be washed in the basin of water provided before meals were served. Saturday was hair washing day.. In summer this was done outside with a large tin bath placed on a chair. As well as washing the hair it was inspected for nits, this meant having it combed with a sharp tooth comb for hours. Boys all had short hair but most girls didn't have their hair cut until they were teenagers so the hair was usually dry by the time this was finished.

On Saturday nights a part of the kitchen was curtained off, the tin bath was filled with hot water so everyone could have a bath. So there was always plenty of water for the important things.

The houses were always clean inside and outside no matter what size or shape they were. The owners were proud of them and outsides got painted or whitewashed once a year. Inside got wallpapered. The most important thing about these houses was that there was always a warm welcome for everyone who called.

Pocket Money

Pocket money wasn't something we got every week. We usually had to earn any money we got from parents or friends.

There were many different ways to earn some pennies. When we did get some we were determined to get "value for money" when it came to spending it. We were always ready to fetch water from the pump or other goods from the shops for neighbours or elderly people. Of course we were told not to expect payment for helping others and we respected this rule. Sometimes we would get rewarded with sweets or homemade buns and sometimes with money.

Picking blackberries was another way we got money. Sometimes we were also allowed to go potato picking. This was done in October or November when the weather was very cold. The farm we went to was quite a bit away and we only got to go with older people. The potatoes were grown in "drills" in large fields. A man went in front with a plough drawn by a horse. The plough dug them out of the ground. Then the "pickers" followed with buckets and when the buckets were full we carried them to the "pits". These were situated at the bottom, middle and top of the fields. We worked from ten o'clock until one o'clock and then we all went into the farm house for dinner. It was usually large plates of Irish Stew or Bacon and Cabbage with lots of potatoes of course, by then we would have eaten anything. Then at two o'clock we went back to the field and worked away until five. Because I was still at school I was only allowed to do this on Saturday, but we enjoyed it and got shillings instead of pennies for it. Most of which we had to save for Christmas.

Whenever we got money given to us it was always with the same advice "don't spend it all in one shop". That was the one bit of advice we obeyed. Our spending spree started at the sweet shop at the bottom of the town and we worked our way to the top. Can you imagine five girls with sixpence each? We had to sample everything. Ice cream was usually too expensive as it was sold at two pence per wafer, so that was passed. Our favourite shop was right at the top of the street and the lady who owned it had "the patience of Job" to put up with us. The shop was like Aladdin's cave filled with all types of sweets. As you entered the shop there were shelves all around holding up glass jars filled with hundreds of sweets. In front was a glass counter that contained most of the "penny sweets". There were penny toffees, liquorice pipes, liquorice laces, broken crunchies (6 pieces for one penny), bull's eyes, pear drops, lemon sherbets and many more. So many that we were spoilt for choice and as we wanted to try all of them it took us ages to decide, but she never rushed us. Everyone's favourite was the broken chocolate bars. In that jar were so many pieces of chocolate and we got five pieces for one penny. If the lady put in a large piece we would ask her to exchange it for two smaller pieces and she would. When the final choice was made and paid for we left. Then we had more fun swapping our sweets on the way home.

Sunday Afternoon

Sunday afternoons were our times of freedom, dinner over, house work done and the rest of the day was left to enjoy doing our own thing.

First step was the shop, where we bought as many sweets as we could afford. Then groups of happy girls would head out of town towards the forest. The forest walk was always very enjoyable and interesting, with all the different trees and flowers. Our first stop was usually the wishing well where we would make a cup from laurel leaves and use it to drink the cool spring water while making a wish. These wishes were secret, but we enjoyed discussing the previous wishes that were made the week before, and express our delight or disappointment depending on whether they were granted or not.

The walk continued on to Cromwell's Bridge, The Lady's Lake, Sarah's Bridge, The flax mill, and the Ice house. These places were steeped in history and legend. Some of which we learned at school, others were retold many times by story tellers on winter nights as they sat around the fires. Rabbits, foxes, squirrels, mink, hares and lots more small animals that we didn't know the names of would run across our paths or just hide and look out at us as we walked by.

There were also lots of birds flying around with as many more just sitting in the trees singing.

Living so close to the forest the local people had many stories about things that happened there over the years, not all true but interesting.

There were the stories we would listen to in neighbour's houses on winter evenings.

For instance it was told that the Ice house was

bottomless, and we often heard about all the unusual things that were dumped there over the years from human bodies to dead animals and even the money taken from the local bank. We first threw lots of stones into it hoping to hear them hit the bottom but we never did.

There were romantic stories told about Sarah who had a bridge named after her.

There were also stories told about the battles fought at Cromwell's Bridge and all the men who were killed in disputes over land and women.

Also tales of women and children who disappeared in the forest and were never found, we were led to believe that it was their ghosts who wandered there at night,but we never stayed late enough to discover if this were true as not.

The Lady's lake was a favourite place of ours in both winter and summer.

In summer when the flowers and trees were looking their best you could count forty shades of green there and in winter when the water froze solid, it became the local skiing rink.

On other Sundays some walks would take us to Cabra Castle which was a beautiful old castle hundreds of years old. For most of them years it was owned by the Pratt family as were the forest and most of the buildings in town. It was closed then when we visited as most of that family were dead and just two people were employed as caretakers, one was a lady who lit fires and did the cleaning everyday. The other was a man who lived in a flat over the stables, as he lived on his own and didn't have much work to occupy him, he was always delighted to have us visit.

During the war years he made "Clogs" (Wooden shoes) and showed us how he did that, He was the proud owner of a gramophone and lots of records, which he played for us and we practised dancing, luckily there weren't any horses in the stables below as they would have bolted from all the noise we made.

It was considered a great privilege to get entrance to the Castle and we really enjoyed our Sunday visits. Years later, Dun-a-Ri forest park was developed with walking trails all sign posted and Cabra Castle became a very famous Hotel and with its beautiful surroundings was very popular for Weddings and holidays, quite different from when we enjoyed our Sunday walks.

In later years the Wishing well became a tourist attraction after a local lady was inspired by the unusual chestnut tree standing at the entrance.

This was a magnificent tree, about thirty feet high with branches five to ten feet wide growing from all sides and sweeping down to the ground. When we were young we loved playing hide and seek there and we climbed it from every angle, but never reached the top. We often looked like monkeys swinging from the branches. This tree was breath taking all the year around, but when in full bloom it looked like a bride in her wedding dress.

The song "Dun-na-Ri" was recorded by many famous singers and people came from all over Ireland and other countries as it was the perfect place for a picnic, "underneath the spreading chestnut tree". Another rout we took out of town led to the "Lough-an-Lea" mountain, this was quite a long way but we always seemed to have so much to talk and laugh about that we didn't consider it far. When we reached the mountain and climbed up and reached the Cairn top, it was really worth it, as the view was breath taking, six counties could be seen from there. It was one of the most beautiful views anywhere in Ireland. This mountain was situated in the town land of Muff which was also famous for the annual Horse fair.

Remembering

Looking back on my childhood, having lots of money or not having much didn't seem to matter. People who were well off didn't act any differently than those who were poorer. As children we were never aware of the difference, we never went cold or hungry. People even shared their knowledge. We were made welcome at tennis matches, badminton, handball and the adults were always willing to teach us the games. We were also welcome to the suppers afterwards, where we were given tea and lots of homemade cakes and buns.

Football was the only game that girls were not allowed to play with the boys. We were welcome at the matches though as we took care of the boys clothes because there were no dressing rooms. We also had to retrieve the ball when it came across the wire, this was very important as only one ball was available for each match. Occasionally when the home team was being beaten, the ball accidentally got burst, the game got cancelled and replayed at a later date that usually suited the home team.

In summer as well as bringing tea to the men working in the hay fields, we enjoyed the rides on the hay cart and the horses while bringing the hay home. On summer evenings we accompanied our parents to the wood. While we played among the trees as they collected fire wood. When it was time to go home we were each given some wood to carry, this was often the only source of fuel.

The adults made a social occasion of these outings, exchanging news and gossip, enjoying being together. The games we played when young were simple but enjoyable. Boys played cowboys and Indians, enjoying making lots of noise. Marbles was another game, roller skating, hop scotch as well as badminton, tennis and football. Girls enjoyed most of these games as well as playing with dolls and prams. We were lucky enough to have a cinema in town and Saturday mornings would see it filled with children. It was usually western films that were shown then. That's when we first got acquainted with Roy Rogers, Gene Audrey and other cowboys as well as their horses. Nine pence got us seats at the front. We were glued to the screen, living every move with the actor, ever diving underneath the seats when the shooting started. It seemed so close we were afraid we would get shot. We acted out the film over and over all week.

Later on the cinema became a dance hall on Saturday nights. This was accomplished by the removal of the front seats to leave room for dancing. It worked like that for many years. The girls had to wait for the boys to ask them to dance, so it was a long walk for the boys up through the seats and very embarrassing going back down if the girls said no.

The summers seemed to pass very quickly as there was so much to do. In winter we passed the evenings by listening to the radio or records played on the gramophone. The adults played cards and told ghost stories, when the snow came we built snowmen and played snowballing. When it was freezing we put water on the lanes and spent many happy hours sliding down on bags and on upturned stools. Children from other parts of town joined us, young and old.

Halloween was always an exciting time, we played trick-a-treat and enjoyed the fruits and nuts we got on our rounds. We enjoyed the "tricks" more than the people we played them on. After opening their doors many times to find it was a trick they brought out a jug of water and we had to make a quick get away. We were so occupied that the winters passed as quickly as the summers. Boredom was unknown.

Places of Wonder and Magic

As children growing up in a small town, we had freedom to go where we liked, very few places were out of bounds. One place I loved to spend time was the Blacksmiths' Forge.

It was just one large stone built room, with a big open fire on one wall, a large bath of water to one side and a massive anvil in the centre. The fire was fuelled by coal and kept lit day and night. It was kept burning bright by means of a bellows. This consisted of an iron tube underneath the fire, attached to a wheel built into the wall. When the wheel was turned it sent air through the tube which kept the fire burning.

I would sit for hours, watching the blacksmith start with a bar of iron, which he placed in the fire until it was red hot. Then he removed it, plunged it into the cold water and then put it onto the anvil, where he hit it with a massive hammer, bending it into shape.

This was repeated many times until he got the shape he wanted.

When it was a horseshoe shape the horse was brought in. He had his hoof cleaned, the old flesh cut off before the new shoe was placed on his hoof .First to get an imprint , then back into the fire, then the water , finally when it was the right shape and size , nailed to the horse's foot.

To me it was magic, seeing a bar of iron become a horse's shoe. I felt so important when I was allowed to "Blow the Bellows" and keep the fire going. People dropped in all the time and they had wonderful stories to tell.

When it was time to go home I was as black as coal and reeked of smoke. When I reached home I wasn't allowed inside until I washed off as much of the dirt as possible. Then when I got inside, another basin of water, soap and towels where handed to me. I had to strip off all my clothes and wash all over before getting clean clothes. Needless to say it wasn't prayers my mother was saying while all of this was happening.

Another place I loved to spend time was with the carpenter. This man specialised in making carts for horses. His workshop was at the bottom of his house, which was just across from ours. It wasn't always that I got in to watch him as he was very temperamental. Only two children were allowed in at the same time. We would usually have to go to the shop for bread, milk or whatever he was short of before he would let us stay. I thought it was worth it just to watch him start with a piece of timber, cut it into lots of different sizes and after hours of cutting, planeing, and shaping he got what he wanted. No machines, all done with hand held saws, sharp knives and planes (a wooden base with blades inserted at the bottom). After working for hours while we sat on the floor in heaps of sawdust and wood cuttings he collected all the pieces and formed them in to wheels or other parts of the cart.

He worked away every day for weeks until he had a complete cart, it was painted, put together like a jigsaw puzzle and then sold.

I was still dirty and dusty when I got home, but not as bad as after the forge.

The third unusual place we loved to sit when we were allowed was in the mill.

This was a two storied building outside town where oats and wheat were brought from the farms to be dried, crushed and turned into meal and flour. On the top floor the oats and wheat were spread out and had to be turned several times a day so it was dried evenly. On the bottom floor was a large "kiln", this was a huge fire that had to be kept lit night and day and was filled by sawdust, not as dirty as the forge but a lovely fire to sit at on a winters evening. Two caretakers were on duty all the time and it became a "celli house" at times. I enjoyed sitting listening to all the news passing from one to the other and the ghost stories, some nights they played cards.

If we were there at tea break we were given a cup of tea and home made bread, it always tasted better than any I got at home. Usually I had some friends with me when visiting these places, we really thought we were in wonderland and we felt privileged to be allowed share these adventures.

Shops

If someone from another planet had come to our town to shop they would have been very confused. The shop with the sign General Drapery would be ok as they could buy ladies, gents and children's clothes including shoes there. Where it said General Hardware again that would be all right as they sold building materials, coal etc. But when they entered the Pubs then the confusion would start. In some pubs the men and women had to separate when they entered. The ladies were directed to a little room called a "snug". The men continued past the grocery counter to the bar. When they wanted to buy a drink for their wife, girlfriend or mother they ordered and paid for it in the bar and it was brought through to the snug. The ladies were served port or sherry, no way would they be served in the bar and definitely no Guinness or spirits. Of course they could leave the snug and proceed to the grocery to do their weekly shopping as most everything was available there, including meal for the hens and oats for the horses. The butchers were as it said on the door. They sold all types of beef and lamb. They always included some suet for frying the steak.

The newsagent sold light groceries like bread, milk, ice cream, and sweets as well as newspapers. Children were very seldom allowed inside the pubs, except one pub. This was the smallest public house in the town and consisted of just one main room. As you entered the bar was on your right and general grocery on the left. As it stayed open after the other shops closed it was convenient for buying bread late at night. Occasionally I would be sent for bread and I hated going in there. I would quietly approach the door, lift the latch, open the door and try to sneak to the left as quickly as possible. I thought that if I didn't look at the men at the bar that they wouldn't see me.

But it never worked like that, they would all turn around and then you would hear: "ah good girl, you're out late", "hello there, are you going to have a pint now that you're here" from another, " hello gersha what's your name" and everyone of them would make a comment and laugh. They thought they were funny but I didn't and I was almost sick from the smell of drink and smoke. Eventually someone would shout "Jim there's a wee lassie here and I don't think it's a pint she wants, you'd better come out to her". By then I would be so nervous that I almost forgot what I was there for. Of course all the men had to shout "good bye" and comments like "mind yourself now", "hope you're not too drunk", "don't fall off your bike on the way home", "look out for the guards" when I was leaving. I was so glad to get outside and hoped that I wouldn't have to repeat that "shopping experience" for a long time again.

My Parents

My parents were average, at this time the men worked at whatever job they could get if they didn't have a trade. Women stayed at home to take care of the children and used whatever skills they had to earn extra money. For example, knitting, sewing, crocheting and if they were farmers wives selling eggs, milk and butter. My mother and father met and got married in Scotland. They had five children before returning to Ireland where they had three more children. The only work my father could get was as a farm labourer. That meant he had to live with the farmers who employed him, my mother was left to take care of the children. They lived in a rural cottage at first, two miles outside the town. In order to get money for food she got work as a cleaner in the local bank and also the Garda barracks.

This involved walking two miles to town, work started at six thirty. She had to leave the children in care of the eldest girl while she was away. Locking them into one room for safety until she got home. By the time I came along they were living on the "hill" .Life was easier as some of my brothers and sisters were working in London and Dublin, so they sent money home, also parcels of clothes which caused much excitement. Any that didn't fit me could be remade and were passed on to other children. My mother left school at fourteen but worked with a dressmaker for two years before going to Scotland. She was quite good with the sewing machine; she also educated herself by reading. A lot of people never learned to read or write then so she was always in demand for reading letters, filling in forms etc.

Murder was very uncommon in Ireland then, but there was one that I remember very well. A man was accused of shooting his wife in the kitchen of her house. This happened in a town twenty miles away from us but the trial was very big news. When the trial started the newspaper was brought to our house for my mother to read. About ten people came along every night eager to hear the progress of the trial. I think it lasted two weeks before he was found guilty.

She was very good at knitting and crochet, so she was able to earn some extra money this way. I once counted twelve crochet berets in church that she had made; they were big in fashion then. She also had a good singing voice, as had the man next door. So many nights were spent listening to both of them. She would sing a song and everyone in both houses sat and listened, the same happened when he sang. The walls were so thin that it was easy to hear both of them. The lovely songs that I heard then are begin repeated now and recall many happy memories for me when I hear them.

I don't know how she did it but she always made Christmas special. The week before everyone had to help in cleaning the house inside and out. The walls outside got whitewashed and wallpaper was renewed inside. There was always plenty to eat and drink and presents for everyone.

My father was a quiet hardworking man, but his work kept him away from home a lot. He usually got to visit once a month when he brought cattle to the fair. That was when he got to call and bring his wages to my mother. When he was at home, between jobs, he made sure that the garden was fully planted with potatoes and vegetables. He encouraged me to grow flowers and taught me how to take care of them. I was privileged to get the first of the new potatoes and vegetables. At the bottom of our garden was a bog hole and he made turf there. This was a long drawn out process as he had to stand in water up to his knees and throw out the mud. It was left for days to dry and then moulded into sods. The sods were then built into stacks and again left to dry and harden. When it was completely finished it was brought to the back of the house where it was stacked and provided fuel for the winter.

My mother loved flowers and would take me on walks and teach me the names of all the wild flowers. I have referred to the lovely sharing nature of the people living near to us. One unusual time comes to mind, it was when the lady next door lost the key of her front door, my mother gave her our key as it also opened her door.

That meant that the only time our door was locked was when everyone was in for the night and the bolts were put on.

I always thought my parents were special but now I know that all the people who lived on the hill were very special.

The Radio

The radio sat on a special shelf beside the Sacred Heart Altar in our house. It was the only source of communication available in the 1940s and 1950s and was treated with respect. We were lucky to have one, the source of its powers came from two batteries, one dry and one wet, the wet one was filled with distilled water and had to be taken to the garage every week to be refilled. The radio was turned on at one o clock every day for the news and left on for the "sponsored" programmes; they catered for the music lovers, mostly Irish songs and music. Every Tuesday and Thursday we had "Dear Frankie", this was like an "Agony Aunt". People wrote to Frankie telling her about all their problems, trusting her to solve them.

The children were usually sent out side or told to leave the room when this was on, while the adults stayed and listened to every word. It is hard to imagine Irish Dancing on the radio, but it happened.

A programme called "Take the floor", presented by "Din Joe", consisting of traditional Irish music and dance was very popular in every house as anyone who could sing or dance joined in on the kitchen floor. The high light of the week was the football match on Sunday. All the neighbours' gathered in our house to listen to the big game, often there were as many outside as inside, some brought their own chairs and stools, especially if Cavan were playing. Every kick of the ball added to the excitement and for the people listening in it was as good as being in Croke Park. In the evenings the teenagers came along to listen to the "top twenty" and their kind of music from the pirate stations. With the coming of electricity and modern technology the size and sound of the radio changed, now they are fitted into all cars and are so small that they can be carried in coat pockets, but local radio is still a very important way of communication in rural Ireland.

Even though we have fax, email, web and phones, people still use radio to get across messages or complaints and to get the local obituaries and even play bingo. It still plays an important place in the modern world as it is listened to by thousands of people all over the world and for keeping in contact with Ireland and family and friends via the web, and is used to send special greeting both ways. In the days when two batteries were needed to power the radio, it was usual to see people coming into town every weekend carrying a wet battery to be refilled. One gentleman came in every Saturday carrying two batteries on the handle bars of his bike, as children we were very puzzled by this and often asked why he had two, we were first told it wasn't our business to know so we assumed he was very rich and had two radios. It was years later that I discovered that he was a potheen maker and this was his way of transporting it into the pubs in town. He did this for years and as far as I know he never got caught.

The Lights of Home

Electricity didn't come to our town until the late 40's and early 50's, so the source of light in our house came from a paraffin oil lamp. These lamps came in all sizes. The bottom part consisted of a bowl which held the oil and had a "wick" in which the oil travelled to the head. When lit this provided the light, a glass globe was then placed on it and that spread the light around the room. The globe got black from the smoke made by the oil and needed cleaning every day. As it was made from very fine glass this was a very delicate operation. First a piece of very soft cloth was attached to a small stick and this was pushed inside the globe and slowly moved around to remove the smoke stain. Then newspaper was used to shine the glass, one wrong move and the glass would break, needless to say children weren't allowed to do the cleaning.

The lamp was usually hung on a wall in the centre of the room so that the light reached every corner. Candles were used for going from room to room.

The kitchen was the room that everyone gathered in, especially on winter's nights. People visited each other then a lot more than they do now. Our house was known as a "ceilie house", every night it was full of people and there was always a lovely glowing fire. Women brought their knitting and sewing and worked at it while exchanging gossip. The men sat smoking pipes and usually brought the evening paper for my mother to read out loud. When they didn't have tobacco for their pipes they put dried tea leaves into the pipe and smoked that like cigarettes. They also made cigarettes from dried tea leaves rolled in newspaper. Very few women smoked but of course we children copied them making and smoking tea leaves when nobody was around. It usually made us sick so one try was enough.

Other nights the adults played cards, while the children played "ludo" or "snakes and ladders". We also did reading, sewing and knitting as well. Occasionally anyone who could was asked to sing or dance.

We were given some bread and long toasting forks and we toasted the bread by the open fire, everyone enjoyed tea and toast. We also toasted apples this way. Early in the night bricks would be placed in the centre of the fire. When they were hot they were wrapped in old sheets or towels and placed one in each bed, like hot water bottles.

The radio was seldom put on at night as people preferred to talk to each other. Some nights records were played on the gramophone and everyone joined in the sing song. When bedtime came we were vey reluctant to leave, but knowing that the hot bricks had warmed our beds and that there would be a repeat "ceilie" the next night sent us off happy and tired.

First Communion

The preparation for First Communion seemed to go on forever when I was a child. I suppose when you are six years old, two years seems forever. Every day at school all we seemed to do was learn prayers and catechism over and over again, not only at school but at home as well. Questions such as, who is God? Who were his mother and father? Who were the divine persons? And so on. Then every week we had a test, all questions had to be answered word for word as in the catechism. There were lots of slaps and lots of tears before we got it right. I am sure it wasn't easy for the teachers either. With the priest dropping in for spot test unexpectedly and expecting us to be word perfect. Anyway when I think back it was worth it for the pride and joy we felt when the real test came and we all passed with flying colours and got our certificates.

The next weeks flew by, there was so much to do, shopping for new white shoes, socks, underwear and hair ribbons. The white dress had to be got as well but it was usually borrowed, as only rich people could afford new. So all the neighbours brought dresses from house to house until one was found that fitted and looked good. The veil and headdress usually came with the dress and were a perfect match. It didn't matter that they were worn before. First Communion usually took place on a Saturday. So on Friday we were all brought from school to the church to make our First Confession, we didn't even know what sin was, but we had to tell all our faults to the priest and get forgiveness.

The excitement built up until early on Saturday, it was time to get dressed for the big day. It was the first time for most of us to be dressed like princesses. I don't remember much about the actual ceremony, but I remember all the parents being so proud of all the children and the sun shone all day. We all visited our neighbours, Aunts and Uncles. We got money in each house and we thought we were millionaires. This was the first time that we had so much money of our own to spend as we liked. That was just what we did, buying as many sweets and as much ice cream we could and enjoyed every bite. Bed was very welcome that night but it was a day to remember for the rest of our lives.

Easter

I always remember Easter as being a lovely time of the year (and still do). It was more like the start of a new year than the cold dark days of January. Every where there were new beginnings .Leaves appeared on trees, primroses and daffodils were in full bloom underneath the trees and the fields were full of new born lambs playing. Baby chicks were hatching out in tea chests in farm kitchens. Easter being a religious feast, most people went to confessions on Easter Saturday and early mass on Easter Sunday morning. A tradition for the children on Easter Saturday was to go collecting the Easter "Cludog". This consisted of visiting all the farm houses near us and getting fresh hen eggs. When it was time to return home we had at least a dozen eggs each. Easter Sunday morning was like Christmas as all children got gifts of chocolate eggs, usually sitting in lovely egg cups shaped like birds and animals. After mass and breakfast all the eggs that we collected on Saturday were boiled hard. When they were cold we painted faces on them. After dinner we set off with our mothers to a field outside town, this was usually a field with a hill in it. All the eggs were rolled down the hill and each child had to find their eggs. When we were tired running a fire was lit and pots of water boiled for making tea. So we all enjoyed our picnic of hard boiled eggs, bread, tea and sweets sitting on the grass. Returning home tired but happy we would pick some of the lovely daffodils to remind us of Easter Sunday. In large towns an Easter parade was held with the men dressed in their best suits and bowler hats and gloves. The ladies wore beautiful long dresses with high boots and hats (that were called Easter bonnets). The parade was led by the local band and it was a great honour to get the prize for the nicest Easter bonnet.

The Fair Day

The 1st Tuesday of the month was the only day I started for school early, that was Fair Day in our town.

On that day the farmers brought their cattle and pigs to town to be sold. Two men called "Drovers" walked them from the farm, sometimes 6 miles to town. They started off at daylight and as often as not one wild cow would jump the ditch into a field for a mouthful of fresh grass. One drover would have to go after it and find a gate to open to get her back with the rest. When they reached town a good spot was found to show off the herd. The bottom end of town by the church wall was reserved for the pigs.

The noise and smell in town that day is something I'll never forget. Hundreds of cattle on Main Street with steam rising from them and surrounded by cow dung. When the buyers arrived the selling started. They walked around the cattle, poking them with a stick, checking their eyes and teeth.

Then turning to the farmer saying "That's a scrawny lot you have today. How much are you looking for them?"

Farmer "Where are your eyes, that's the best herd of cattle here today. They were fed of the best all year."

Buyer "I'll take them off your hands, if the price is right"

Farmer "£5 each, not a penny less."

Buyer "I would be doing you a favour giving you £1."

Farmer "You'll wait a long time before you get them for that."

Buyer "All right so."
And he walks away. The farmer goes into the eating house for a mug of tae. They both return.

Buyer "Will you come down a bit?

Farmer "Seeing its you, I'll let you have them for £4.

Buyer "I just bought the best of cattle from Jim Smith for £2, I'm willing to give you the same."

Up comes John Kelly saying "Good luck to the work, have you a deal?"
Farmer "He is making little of my herd by offering me £2 and me looking for £4."
John "They're good enough looking cattle. How about splitting the difference? £3 and a luck penny."

Buyers "Fair enough, here shake on it."
They both spit on their hands and then shake and the deal is done.

Both men "Thanks John, there will be a few pints in Gartlands for you."

I am standing enjoying all this until my Uncle asks why I am not at school. I run as fast as I can, through the cattle. Until I realise that I am bringing the smell with me. I look down to see my shoes covered in cow dung. I wash them in a pool of water and continue running to school, thinking up a good excuse for being late.
No matter how many fair days I saw, they all left a special memory with me.
Everything is so different now with closed in marts.

The Carnival

Everyone joined in the celebrations every summer when the annual carnival came to town. It was run as a fund raising event so anyone that could helped to make it enjoyable and profitable. The setting up of the Marquee was usually the first job and took about a day to erect. All the dances were held in it. Then the funfair came consisting of bumping cars, chair-o-planes, swings, swing boats, shooting gallery, hoopla and lots of side shows.

We children didn't have money for all the games but we overcame that by always being available to help the crew by holding ropes, going to the shops, making tea, etc.

In return we got free rides as payment. The days weren't long enough to fit everything in. In the marquee the dancing started at nine o'clock and continued until twelve. All the big name dance bands played and had full houses all week. The committe ladies spent every day baking buns and cakes and making sandwiches to sell in the tea room as well as feeding the band members. The lucky children were the ones who had a family member on the committee as they were brought along to help make the sandwiches and set up the tables. After spending hours buttering bread and helping with refreshments we were allowed to sit quietly at the back, watching the dancing and enjoying the music. It was worth the hours spent spreading butter on bread and then scraping it off again. Then we had to help with the teas and washing up afterwards.

By being in the kitchen we got to meet the members of the bands (some of them quite famous), have photos taken with them and the really nice ones bought sweets for the helpers. The love of music and dance stayed with us for the rest of our lives.

Needless to say school didn't see much of us that week and that led to more excitement when our teachers disagreed with both our mothers and the organising committee members.

The teachers accused the parents of keeping the children away from school in order to help. We just sat back and enjoyed the clash of tempers; it was as good as a concert. It is a true saying that all good things come to an end. We were very sad at the end of that week when everything was dismantled and ready to move on to the next town. Of course we were ready again to help and got paid for same. So at the end of a week of entertainment we had money in our pockets.

When the lorry started leaving town we were really sorry to see them go and followed for some distance but we always had next year to look forward to and lots of stories to tell our friends when we returned to school.

Confirmation

We thought the preparations for First Communion were hard but we didn't know about Confirmation then. The lead up to Confirmation wasn't very enjoyable, for months beforehand at school. We had to learn prayers, catechism and the Bible, drummed into us everyday and we were expected to do it all over again every evening at home. Then every week we had a prayer test, catechism test and bible test. Staying away from school on test day didn't work because when you went back the teacher made you stand in front of the class. She asked you every question and if you didn't answer all of them correctly as well as slaps she embarrassed you by relating the history of all your family.

When the teacher was explaining the ceremony to us, she told us that the bishop would ask each one of us a question. That was the reason we had to know all the answers. If we didn't know the answers to the questions we were asked, we were led to believe we would have to leave the church without getting Confirmation. We were also told that the Bishop would give each of us a slap on the cheek. Well this information made us all very nervous as we had four sisters in the class and none of them liked getting slaps. When the teacher slapped one of them, she ran home to tell her mother and father, they lived close to the school. Then after a few minutes another would leave to look for her sister and within fifteen minutes all four would have gone home. They usually returned some time later with parents in tow demanding to know why their girls had to leave school and why they were upset. Anyway we all had visions of this happening on confirmation day when the Bishop would give his slap.

But it didn't happen as it was explained to them that the Bishop's slap wouldn't hurt, like teacher's did. When the big day arrived it was very exciting. The boys looked quite grown up in lovely suits for the first time, they wore long trousers. The girls had new white dresses with hats and gloves; they felt very important as everyone admired them. My dress was made by my Mother; it consisted of a pleated skirt with a plain top and a lovely bolero and was made from linen. We didn't get many cards, just rosary beads, prayer books and medals. But friends and family gave us money to spend as we wished. The new clothes were put away that evening and only came out to be worn to mass on Sundays. The first Sunday I got to wear my beautiful dress I was allowed to keep it on after mass, later that evening I went cycling with some of my friends. Everything was fine until the front wheel of the bike went into a pot hole, I was thrown in to a pool of dirty water and the white dress turned black. It took a long time to get courage to go home but when I did and when my mother saw the dress she was speechless. It was one of the very few times I saw her really angry and I couldn't blame her after all her hard work in making it. Anyway when she calmed down she somehow got it cleaned and dyed it blue so I got lots more wear out of it. We had to grow up pretty fast after Confirmation as most of us had to leave school at fourteen years of age and start work. Very few could afford secondary education as it was very expensive. We didn't have much choice of what work we did and were considered lucky if we got any job. The money we earned was always needed at home. All that was available for boys was factory work or farms, they were both hard work and long hours. For girls there were few jobs except housework, which included childminding and all other jobs inside and outside the house. Again the work was hard and the hours long. But we considered ourselves lucky to get any work. Anyone who had sisters or brothers in England or America usually got their fare paid to join them, so it was good bye to Ireland and the start of a new life.

Blackberry Picking

September is the month that blackberries ripen. So after school we children would get a tin and a bucket and set off on the adventure of picking blackberries. When we found a good field with lots of briers, we started first by filling the tin and then empting it into the bucket. We went from field to field until the bucket was full then it was time to go home. Next day we brought all the blackberries up town to a shop to sell them. First they were weighted and we got paid by the pound, sometimes a little water was added to make them weigh a bit more.

Jam, ink and dye for clothes were made from the blackberries. We usually got to spend some of the money and saved the rest for when we needed shoes or clothes. Sometimes the money was needed for food or things for the house.

That doesn't seem very exciting or adventurous. The exciting days were when we found an orchard on our travels. By climbing across the wall and climbing the trees we could indulge in as much fruit as we could eat. If the owners came along with his dogs we usually crossed the wall much quicker on the way out. Other times the famers wife would find us, treated us to tea and scones at the kitchen table and give us eggs and homemade butter to bring home. Some days we were accompanied to the fields by adults. Instead of blackberries they would fill our buckets with turnips or cabbage that were growing in the fields and a few blackberries

would go on top. The owners of the vegetables were aware of this but didn't mind sharing them. What we brought home was also shared with our neighbours and friends. That was the way people survived then, all helping each other.

Trips out of Town

Travelling wasn't available to most people but they didn't seem to mind, not visiting other places. I was lucky as I got my first train ride when I was about nine years old.

Some of our relations were on holiday about ten miles from us, so my mother took me by the train to visit them. We had to walk for a mile to the railway station and the same when we got to the end of the journey, but the long walk were worth it as going on a train was very exciting and a lot of people never got to do that in their life time. Another time we made the same journey by bus, this was a very different experience as the bus travelled a different route than the train and made many stops for people to get on and off. The driver seemed to know all the passengers and he delivered the daily papers to shops in every town that we went through. About that time a business couple who had three children asked my mother if she would allow me to go to their house after school to help the mother with the children. She agreed on conditions that I was happy about doing it and that I would not be expected to do all the house work. They provided my dinner and tea everyday and as they had a car we were taken for drives every Sunday. The couple were lovely but with three children I was kept busy. I helped with the changing and feeding of the younger two, this was my first time to give a baby a bottle and I was so scared of choking her. It was also the first time I changed a nappy and when I was presented with a very dirty smelly one I just got sick. I swore that I would never do that again. I remember the mother laughing and telling me that I would soon get used to it when I had children of my own I vowed that I would never have children if they came with dirty nappies, but of course she was right. Every Sunday we had a day out, most times it was to visit the children's grandparents, Aunts and Uncles. We usually went in time for dinner and always had a good time and lots of fun, on these visits. The Grandparents lived on a farm and before tea time the older children and I went with their children to the fields to bring the cows in for milking. Being fearless we decided we would try to milk the cows, there was one very quiet cow, so we always practised on her and she stood quietly and let us. Long afterwards we heard the Grandfather and Uncles expressing their worries about this cow as her milk yield dropped at week-ends of course we sat and pretended that we didn't know what they were talking about. Other Sundays in the summer we got taken to the seaside, the preparations for these trips stated the day before as extra clothes were needed for all the children also extra food and bottles of milk for the baby and of course plenty of nappies. As this was before disposables and plastic bags a bucket with a lid had to be included for the soiled nappies. All the food we needed for the day was also packed. The only thing that was purchased at the seaside was ice cream. We always seemed to eat much more on these outings than we did at home and it really tasted better with sand. We spent hours building sand castles and cried when they fell down, just when we had finished them. We played ball on the beach and paddled in the sea until we were exhausted when it was time to pack everything and everyone into the car for the drive home. We were asleep as soon as the car started and we slept all the way home.

When we arrived there were more tears from the younger ones when they were woken up, washed, and got ready for bed.

These are wonderful memories and I appreciate having

a very happy childhood. This family were used to a different lifestyle than mine and I consider myself very lucky to have been part of it. The Grandparents farm was close to a small village that consisted of one general shop, one pub, a school and a church, if the priest had to say an extra Mass during the week he called to this house for some of the children to serve, usually it was a boy, but if they were not available he allowed a girl to help. I had to accompany one of the girls once, and it was very unusually and special as there were only three of us in the church, the priest, the server and me. It was many years later that girls were allowed to serve at Mass.

Two types of milk

Every morning before breakfast I was given a jug and three pence and sent across the road for a pint of milk. The cows were milked twice a day, morning and night. The older children had to do the milking before going to school; it was all hand milking then.

The milk was brought into the pantry (a type of cold room). It was then strained into a crock; this was a large earthenware bowl that kept the milk cold. A pint measure was then lowered into the milk, when full it was lifted out and the milk poured into my jug. The pint measure was like a cup made out of tin with a long handle. The milk that wasn't used in the house or sold was kept in the crock until cream started to form on the top. It was then transferred into a churn; this was a container like a barrel with a dash and a lid. The dash was round at the bottom with holes cut into it. It had a long handle which the lid fitted over. The milk was churned by moving the dash up and down for several hours. Salt and cold water were added at intervals until butter was removed and moulded into shape with butter platters. Some was sold and the rest was used by the family. The milk left in the churn was called buttermilk; it made a refreshing drink and was also used in bread making.

Up the road from us Maggie and her family depended on two goats for their supply of milk. These goats wore necklaces around their necks made from the rims of buckets. These necklaces were then tied together with ropes and were meant to stop the goats wandering, it didn't always work.

Maggie kept them in the back garden but occasionally they escaped into next door's garden. They helped themselves to cabbage, potatoes and everything else they could eat, even clothes off the line. Needless to say when they were discovered all hell broke loose. The neighbour arriving at Maggie's door dragging the goats with them, very angry of course. When the shouting died down Maggie promised that she would make sure it didn't happen again.

That was alright until next time when they went into the front garden, where they dined on all the flowers including the rose bushes which were just in bloom. Then there were three or four ladies at Maggie's door plus the goats and it was like world war three, the goats were very lucky to survive. The fallout lasted for weeks usually until there was a shortage of milk and then the goats were back in favour.

Maggie didn't believe in milking just twice a day as the milk would be used up as quickly as it was brought home. So when ever she made tea she just went to the back door and shouted "here kiddie, here kiddie, here kiddie" and no matter how far away they were they came running to her. This also happened when visitors called and were invited to stay for tea. When she brought the milk in she strained it through a piece of muslin cloth and then, to cool it added cold water, poured it into a jug and took it straight to the table. The visitor didn't know that it was goat's milk they were drinking or how fresh it was.

Goat's milk was always considered better than cow's milk for children so that's the reason all the children who got goat's milk when they were young were healthy and happy.

Christmas

Christmas in the 40's and 50's were a lot different from what they are today. Firstly there wasn't the same amount of money at the time and a lot less things to buy, but the preparations and excitement was just as good as now. People made the best of what they had and for the children it was still magic.

For my mother the important things to get done at Christmas were to whitewash the house outside and wallpaper inside then the cooking. She always made her own plum puddings and everyone helped. All the fruit, currants, raisins and sultanas had to be rolled in flour to clean them. Lemons and Oranges were grated and juice squeezed out. Bread got grated and made into breadcrumbs. Eggs were whisked until they were light and fluffy and lard melted over a pot of boiling water, so everyone had a job to do. When all the ingredients were ready they went into a large bowl and mixed together, after that the mixture was wet with beer and milk.

A large wooden spoon was then used to mix it all together, everyone in the house and those who called had to have a stir and make a wish. Then the whole lot was put into a sweet can lined with greased proof paper, covered well and then put into a pot of boiling water and left to boil for eight hours. For Christmas dinner we usually had a turkey, some people preferred a goose or duck. There were always lots of potatoes and vegetables as they were home grown. Christmas morning was always exciting as there was always presents for all.

Boys got cowboy suits complete with hat and guns, footballs, marbles, farmyard animals and sweets.

For the girls there was doll, prams, skipping ropes, tea sets, books and of course sweets.

All the children usually got new clothes, shoes, trousers, dresses and socks. The Christmas stockings left at the bottom of the bed on Christmas Eve were not forgotten. It usually had an apple, orange, sweets and small toys in it from Santa.

Now the presents are bigger and more expensive but the excitement and joy was just the same years ago. The day started with everyone going to church and exchanging season's greetings with each other. After dinner the road filled with children and toys. Everything was brought out to be shared with each other and nobody noticed what the weather was like.

The fair of Muff

A walk to the Loc-an-Lea mountain at any time was very enjoyable and provided many a pleasant memory, but on the 12th of August every year was different as this was the date that the annual Fair of Muff was held. Hundreds of people travelled from all parts of Ireland, England and some from the U.S.A. for this annual horse fair.

The fair of Muff dates back to the 17th century, it is also known as the pattern fair.

There are other Annual fairs held in Ireland, but Muff has grown and seems to have a special magic of its own, and attracts people from near and far. The horse sales are held at the cross roads, but the day takes on a carnival style as soon as you start down the narrow road to the left, there you will find it thronged with stalls selling everything from a needle to an anchor.

As children we saved any money we got for weeks before hand to spend at Muff. Stall holders travelled for days from every part of Ireland to Muff, some camping there over night and the fair day was like an unofficial holiday.

The excitement built up as we moved from stall to stall. There were so many things for sale, including many different types of sweets, we were spoiled for choice. We discovered the way to get value for money was for each of us to buy something different, and then share with each other. That way we got to sample almost every type of sweets that were for sale.

The sweets were sold in cone shaped bags made from news papers. Eventually when we worked our way past all these stalls we arrived at the games area, these were called "games of chance", spin the wheel, spot the lady,

3 card tricks, hoop through, lucky dip etc,.
There were always plenty of gamblers around these games all hoping to make some easy money. Further along the road other games were on going like "Skittles" and Horse shoe throwing", these were team games and very exciting for the teams taking part and their supporters.

A large tent stood nearby, one part sold alcoholic drinks and at the other side you could purchase tea and sandwiches.

Nearby was the Dancing Deck, there a band played all day and couples danced until late.

That walk took you to the bottom of the large rock where the serious gambling took place, this was a game called "Pitch and toss", the idea was to throw two pennies into the air and bets were placed on whether they landed "Heads or Harps",big money was won and lost at this game and some times would lead to fights among people who disagreed with the tosser's decision. It is reported that in the 1800s two men were killed while playing for very big stakes, the fair was banned for two years then, on top of the rock was where you got a birds eye view of the beauty of surrounding country side and towns. Mothers and Children sat there for hours enjoying the view. I don't remember any wet days. The sun always seemed to shine in August then. At the end of the day as we made our way home and arrived at the crossroads ,we stood and watched the reason for it all, that was the buying and selling of horses. There were horses of many breeds, colour and sizes there. They would be vetted up and down many times by the potential buyers before a decision was made.

They would look then go away, look at other horses come back, watch as young boys galloped the horses up and down the road, then they checked the legs and teeth and after asking for another run the haggling would start with the seller pointing out all the good points of the horse and the buyers listing all the bad ones, until we often though it would end in a boxing match as tempers would reach boiling point.

Eventually seller and buyers would agree on a fair price, hands were spat on and then shaken to seal the deal and afterwards the children from both families would benefit from the "Luck Penny". In olden days the fair lasted for a week, with many travelling people coming to Muff several days in advance and each family would set up camp in the same place as in previous years, then horse drawn caravans of many colours were like a rainbow along the roads, to take a jaunt around Killarney in similar ones today would cost the tourist dearly. At night time many local people would visit the travellers around the fire side for a sing-song and to exchange stories. Apart from those who came to trade, others visited for a reunion with family and school friends, many who would not have met for years, were sure to meet at Muff.

At the end of that road the caravans of many colours were parked and it was usually the ladies who sold the home made paper flowers, pots, pans, fire irons and many ornaments made from wood. We usually bought small presents there for parents and other children at home. As we started for home reviewing all the events of the fair we were tired but excited about all our new experiences. When we got offered a lift in one of the beautiful side carts it was just the perfect end to a perfect day and we arrived back in town feeling like royalty.

My First Encounter with Death

When a baby was born in any of the houses on our road it was the custom to bring other children in to see the new baby. The women brought cloths for the baby and cooked food for the mother. Everyone helped with the other children getting them up, washed, dressed and fed before school. There was always someone to take care of them after school until bedtime. It was a very caring neighbourhood. All babies were born at home with the help of the midwife and the neighbours.

One day I returned from school and all I could see were sad faces and everyone talking in whispers. When I asked what was wrong I was told that one of Mrs K's twins had died, a little boy about one month old, his little sister was okay but everyone was grieving as if it was their own. Next day at school all the children were very sad and tearful. So the teachers thought it would help us to deal with it if we went to see the baby. It was arranged that we would meet with the teachers and visit the house at five o'clock. None of us knew what to expect, so we put on brave faces and went in. When we saw the beautiful little boy in his cot we were surprised that he just looked as if he was asleep. We were lined up in a row while he was put into a little white coffin. There were a lot of tears shed by young and old as we walked behind that little white coffin through the town to the church.

A few months later there was another death in the neighbourhood. This time it was a man who was going down a steep hill on his bicycle to work. When he got to the bottom of the hill the breaks on his bike failed to work so he was thrown head first into a wall and died instantly.

The night of the wake my mother brought me with her and I was expecting to see him just like I had seen him everyday looking peaceful like the baby did.

I wasn't prepared for what I saw, he was in bed, but as he had crashed into a wall his face was badly disfigured and was covered in bandages. I got the shock of my life and had nightmares for weeks afterwards.

Emigrants Return

When children reached fourteen years of age it was legal to leave school, there weren't any jobs in Ireland for most so they had to emigrate to England or America. It was easier for them if they already had a brother or sister there as they paid the fare and provided a place to stay. It usually took years of hard work before they saved enough money for the return fare. As well as keeping themselves they sent money home every week. If they went to England it could be five years before they came home. From America it was often twenty years and for some it never happened.

Anyway when they did arrive it was very exciting, as they brought much needed money and it was a party all the time.

People thought they were millionaires and were expected to treat everyone, which they did. The presents they brought were much appreciated, especially by the parents. So there was lots of food for everyone. Neighbours and friends gathered every night to welcome the emigrants, enjoyed the good food and drink and listened to the stories they had to tell about far away lands. It was hard to believe all they heard as it was so different from life in Ireland.

Once we had an American millionaire visit friends on the hill. He arrived in a massive chauffeur driven car. People came from all over just to see the car. It had an Irish flag on one side and the American flag on the other. The car was driven up and down the road every day with the yank throwing money and sweets to all the children who followed as if he was the pied piper.

He had come from America with the idea of buying the

six counties of Ireland back from England. He made headlines in all the papers and met a lot of important people but the deal wasn't done.

It was quiet after the visitors returned to their work but the stories they told were retold over and over again when people got together for months afterwards and looked forward to the next time.

Visiting the Farms

As the hill was situated at the end of town it meant that it was also at the start of the County, so we had the best of both worlds, town on one side with all its conveniences and wide open spaces and forest on the other.

There were two farms we loved to visit, one was a very large old type farm owned by a middle aged couple who had lived there all their lives and as they didn't have children of their own, they were happy for the town children to visit and we always got a very warm welcome from Sam and Millie.

As I had three best friends where one went all four did. They allowed us to help in whatever they were doing when we arrived. We were sent out to the fields for the cows when it was time for milking. We got to hold buckets of milk for the calves to drink; sometimes more milk went over our clothes than into the calves. We just refilled the buckets and started to feed them over again. Feeding the fowl, which consisted of hens, ducks, geese and turkeys, was another job we were asked to do, also collecting the eggs.

In the hen house, large pots and boxes were placed all around the walls and filled with straw most of the hens used these to lay in but some hens laid out, that meant making their own nest in the long grass or usually in the hay shed, it was exciting searching through the hay for the nest. Sometimes we found as many as ten eggs in one nest.

The nests were hidden in the middle of the hay, so Millie didn't always see them, so they were very happy when we brought in all the eggs, as they provided part of their income. The eggs were washed and rubbed all over with soda and sold at the weekend. They both worked very hard from light of day until darkness but they always made time to spend with us when we visited.

After the outside work was finished we went inside for tea, it was a beautiful old house. It had a very large kitchen, with a huge Aga cooker taking up one side of the kitchen. A clothes line stretched over it for drying the clothes, between the cooker and a lovely bay window stood massive pot with a plant. I never did find out the name of the plant, but it stood in the same place for years, occasionally Millie would give us a drink of butter milk or some other home made drink. If we didn't like it we just watered the plant with it, which never stopped it growing. On the next wall was a dresser which held all the delph on the top shelves and the press underneath held the saucepans and buckets.

The centre of the kitchen was occupied by a large table which had a variety of uses meals were prepared and eaten at it, bread made, eggs washed, chickens plucked before cooking and it had lots of other uses. It was really the heart of the kitchen, there was a mixture of seating in the kitchen a few wooden chairs around the table with stools of all sizes placed near the fire along with two large armchairs one each side of the fire. The floor was made of large square of slate, the sitting room, or parlour was very different from the kitchen, this was only used on special occasions or for Christmas dinner.

This room was at the front of the house and had carpet on the floor and very heavy velvet curtains covered the two big bay windows. The fire place was made of marble with a mantle piece full of old ornaments and two large china Blue and White dogs, were placed one each side of the fire. It also contained a beautiful "China Cabinet", filled with the best china tea sets and glasses, a round table in the centre of the room seated twelve and it wasn't used very often.

All these old houses had certain grandeur in their layout. Most had a large sweeping lawn that started at the front door and ended at a river. Beautiful weeping willow trees grow along the banks of the river and usually a large monkey puzzle grew in the centre of the lawn. This provided a fantastic view from the sitting room window. Especially in January and February when the lawn was white with snowdrops and at Easter the lawn became like a sea of yellow when the daffodils were in bloom.

Our tea was taken in the kitchen and we usually got boiled eggs with home made bread and apple tart, and sometimes scones with jam. After our visit to Sam and Millie we returned home tired but happy with lots of fresh milk, eggs and enough vegetables for the following week. We were always given a large bunch of flowers which were placed in the centre of the kitchen table. They brightened up not only the room but brought a smile from all who passed them.

The other farm we enjoyed visiting was nearer the town. We were only allowed to go there on bright summer evenings. Joe, who kept Greyhounds, sent us there to collect milk for his dogs. We had to wait for the Cows to be milked; the milk got strained and then left to cool before it was put into our cans.

This farm house was a regular "ceilie" house for the men from nearby farms as they didn't have TV then. They came together to exchange gossip, news and tell stories. This all happened as we enjoyed tea and currant bread at the kitchen table. On the nights we were there the only stories they told were ghost stories. The adults seemed to enjoy seeing our fear. By the time the milk was ready we were really scared.

We sat opened mouthed as each story was more hair raising than the last. By the time we left for home, our imaginations were working overtime, as every tree that we saw looked like a Ghost.

One night I was the one who nearly killed us all with fright, being summer we were usually bare foot, and as we walked along too scared to even talk I found something moving underneath my foot, I screamed really loud and we all started running as fast as we could. We were near home when we stopped and I was asked why I screamed, everyone thought that I had really seen a Ghost.
We discovered afterwards that it was a frog that I had stepped on. The grey hounds didn't get any milk that night as can and milk were left with the frogs.

Entering the work force

When I finished school I went to work in a local house.
I was employed as a housekeeper but I was expected to
help with all the work. The owners also had a farm and
served dinners on fair days. Most houses on the main
street had a large garden and a yard at the back where
they grew all vegetables and potatoes for use in the
house. The sheds in the yard were used for hens,
turkeys, ducks, pigs and the cattle were housed in the
byers at night. In the mornings after milking, the cows
were driven onto the main street and out to the farms.
They were brought back in at night.

As most people lived the same way it was common to
see herds of cattle been driven through town twice a
day.

There were nine adults living in the house I worked in.
That meant a lot of cooking, cleaning and washing, as
well as feeding the fowl and pigs twice daily.

Every night a large pot of potatoes were washed and put
on the big open fire in the back kitchen to boil. During
that time the milk was strained, eggs cleaned and food
prepared for the next day's dinner. When the potatoes
were cooked they were lifted off the fire and the water
was drained away .Before adding meal to them we took
some and ate them with just butter and salt. Then meal
was added and they were mashed up with a large mallet
and they were ready for morning feed.

At that time most floors were covered by linoleum, this
had to be washed, polished and shined every day, as
well as dusting and bed making.

On the first Tuesday of every month the cattle and pig
fair was held. Farmers brought all animals for sale.
Where I worked they served dinners to the farmers that

day. As many as fifty three course dinners were provided in the dining room. So you can imagine the amount of food that was cooked that day. Most of it had to be prepared the day before, as all was done on one Aga cooker. This work was left to the four ladies in the house and me. They all worked very hard and did long hours every day as did the men, some of whom worked on the farm while others worked in the local factories.

The hours I worked were long but never boring as there were so many different jobs to do and at the end of the week it was good to have money for the cinema and dances. All my friends seemed to work just as hard. I worked there for one year until my mother decided that the work was too hard for me and so I left then.

My next job was also in a town house, in ways similar to the first one. They had large gardens and yard. They also had a farm outside town. A shoe shop and pub were attached to the living quarters and there were seven children in the family.

So some of my work was the same as before and some very different. For instance even though there was a man employed for the outside work I was expected to help there as well as with the house work and the children. For the pub we had to wash all bottles by hand. This was done by first soaking the bottles in cold water and placing them one by one onto a rotating brush. They were then stacked in crates to dry.

The Guinness was delivered in large wooden barrels. The idea was to knock out the wooden plug and attach a tap to the barrel. The bottles were then held underneath until they were full, a cap and label went on to the bottles. Every pub had their own label with their name, address and date of bottling on it. The beer was then left to settle in a cold shed for weeks before been put on the shelves. This work was done in very cold conditions. With seven children to attend as well there wasn't much leisure time but as I wasn't much more than a child myself I enjoyed playing with them. Can you imagine trying to collect all them at tea time. The first two left at the table would be gone by the time two more would be found. So I solved that problem by bringing all the children I could find and placing them in a shed until I had all of them, then I sent all the neighbours children home and fed the rest.

Saturday night bath time was another time hard to co ordinate. It had to be done in relays, two left to soak in the bath while two were been dried and dressed. That worked when everybody was happy but at times when they were overtired rows and tears started and that really upset the routine. Looking back I often wonder how I coped with it all as I was just three years older that the eldest of the children. But I did enjoy my time there as the mother and father were hard workers and were very good to me.

Everyday was different, for instance the pub was known as a footballer's pub. Occasionally I might have to cook breakfast for most of the County team because the meeting the night before over ran and it was too late for them to go home...

Another Happy Memory

Different things bring back memories of special times in my youth. Also different seasons of the year. When I think back to the long hot summer days, it reminds me of the travelling people who returned every summer and set up camp on the outskirts of town. There were two families who came back and usually stayed about a month. They were always made to feel very welcome by the people of the town as they never caused any trouble. They are just people who preferred to live in the open spaces instead of a house. They didn't beg for goods, but used the Barter system, exchanging some items for others. For instance when they needed bread, milk, sugar or tea they called to the houses and instead of payment with money they exchanged saucepans, tin cans, clothes pegs and other things that they made around the camp fire. They were very knowledgeable about herbs and could produce a cure for animals or humans who were ill. Most people respected this way of life and it was considered unlucky to upset them. Sometimes they foretold the future by reading the cards or the tea leaves for this they had to share a cup of tea with the person whose future they were foretelling. My brother took me and my friends to visit the camp fires in the evening and we would sit and watch them making all the items that the women exchanged for food.

Their living quarters were very small just some small tents that they slept in and we often wondered how they all fitted into them as there were children there also.

They did all their cooking and washing outside and for that reason they always set up camp near a river so they always had plenty of fresh water.

They washed the cloths by the river with the help of a

washboard and soap. The hours we spent there seemed to pass very quickly as they were great story tellers and would keep us spellbound by the tales they told. Their teenage boys and girls were very good looking with either beautiful blonde or black haired and they would also entertain us for hours as they sang song after song, most of which we never heard before but like all good songs every one told a story. Their children didn't attend school as they didn't stay very long in one place but all the skills of their parents were passed on to them and in lots of ways they were better educated than those who went to school everyday. They were always very welcome when they visited and we were sad when the time came for them to move on, but we had next year to look forward to.

Teenage Years

When we reach thirteen or fourteen we believe we are really grown up. At last we're "teenagers" and a whole new world is supposed to open up to us. But adults don't see it like that, and they seem to forget our age when it suits them.

If we get upset because we don't get the thing we were promised we are told "stop acting like a child, you're a big girl now". Or if you're going out with friends and you apply some makeup you are told "wash that muck off your face, you're too young for makeup. Time enough for that when you are older". So teenage years can be very confusing. At the same time we are leaving our childhood years behind.

One thing that changes is our wish list. When we are children we wish for simple things, like dinner without carrots or an unexpected day off school, or that teacher won't ask to see our homework because we haven't done it. At Christmas the wish list is all about Santa. Girls wish for that lovely doll with the big blue eyes that close when she sleeps and long blonde hair that we can spend hours styling. Boys wish for footballs, cars, or cowboy suits complete with guns and holster, or farm animals that look just like the real ones. At the time these are the most important wishes we make and we pray that when Santa comes that he won't just bring new clothes and sweets like other years.

When I was fifteen my two greatest wishes were for a watch and a bicycle, two things that were very expensive at that time and very few teenagers got them until they were working and could pay for them with their wages. But I still wished. I said earlier that my mother was a wonderful women and she really proved that and showed that she could make dreams come through. When I was fourteen she bought me a lovely watch and for my sixteenth birthday she got me a bicycle. I better explain how she managed this as she didn't have much money, but she was very good with what she had.

Hire purchase had just been introduced in Ireland and was called "the never never plan" because most people who availed of this method of buying could not afford the repayments. So for years they just paid the interest and never got it all paid off. But my mother some how had the repayments ready every week, so when she had the watch paid for she started paying for the bicycle.

Getting the watch was brilliant as very few of my friends had one but when I got the bicycle it opened up a whole new experience for me. It meant that when I got off work I could visit all other towns within an eight mile radius and discover many things that we didn't have in our town. When I was sixteen I learnt about a family living in another town eight miles from us who were looking for a girl to help with the housework and their children. So being adventurous I phoned for an interview and got an appointment for the following Wednesday. So on my day off work I cycled the eight miles, had the interview and got the job. I started two weeks later and all my neighbours and friends thought I was crazy to leave home and a "good job" and move to a strange town where I didn't know anybody. The only people who left home then went either to USA or England. That was accepted and a going away party was organised for them. The difference was that they didn't get a chance to return to Ireland for many years, while I could cycle home on Wednesdays and Sundays.

The following week I got on my bike and travelled to start my new job and I'm pleased to add that I never regretted that decision.

The family consisted of mother, grandmother, two teenage children and twins aged nine (their dad had died some years before) From day one I was treated as just another member of the family by everyone. Can you imagine how different it was from my previous job. Only two children to take care off instead of eight, no pigs or hens to feed, no Guinness to bottle, no milk to churn. It was like heaven. Everyone in the town was very friendly and I made lots of friends my own age very quickly. When they brought me to their homes I was made very welcome, we were allowed to chat and listen to music in their rooms, and at supper time I was given the same as their own children.

I was really happy there, the work was so much easier and the family were so good to me. They had a business that I wasn't expected to help in. Other people were employed for that. They also had a car and when they took the younger children out for the day I was brought along also.

I got lots of free time, my work finished at seven o'clock every evening, I had a half day on Wednesday and Sunday when I could cycle home. My social life was good also as there was a dance hall and cinema in the town and taxis to take us to the carnival dances in the summer.

My wages were twice what I got in my previous job and when other family members came to dinner on Sunday I got extra "tips" and help with the washing up so that I still had lots of time to go home. From the first day I arrived in that town I considered it home and still do. I think it has remained one of the friendliest towns in Ireland and I have stayed friends with a lot of the people I first met there so many years ago.

I stayed there for three years until I was nineteen and then I got married and moved to England.

That was the start of many more happy memories.

Doonaree

If you ever go to Ireland I'm sure you will agree
To take the road from Dublin town way down to Doonaree
'Tis there you'll find a wishing well beyond a chestnut tree
In a shady nook, by a winding brook
Will you make this wish for me
Oh to be in Doonaree with the sweetheart I once knew
To stroll in the shade of the leafy glade where the rhododendrons grew
To sit with my love on the bridge above the rippling waterfall
But to go back home never more to roam is my dearest wish of all

And if you take the hilly path to the woods where bluebells grow
Where we as barefoot children played so many years ago
You'll find a slumbering castle there enshrined in memory
In a shady nook, by a winding brook
Will you make this wish for me
Oh to be in Doonaree with the sweetheart I once knew
To stroll in the shade of the leafy glade where the rhododendrons grew
To sit with my love on the bridge above the rippling waterfall
But to go back home never more to roam is my dearest wish of all
To go back home never more to roam is my dearest wish of all
back home never more to roam is my dearest wish of all